ROCK CLIMBING

by Kate Cooper

The author

Dr. Kate Cooper first tried rock climbing in 1988 at Yorkshire's Almscliff. In 1999 she began climbing regularly indoors at the Leeds Wall and outside in Yorkshire and Derbyshire. She also likes to climb in Cumbria, Wales, Dartmoor and Spain. Her favourite rock type is rhyolite.

With thanks to: Nick Smith, Keith Sharples, John Cleare, Trudi Webb, Diana LeCore, Marc Adams and Anna Brett

Thank you to Lorraine Petersen and the members of nasen

The author wishes to thank Mick Ryan, Toby Foord-Kelcey, Stuart Anderson and the many helpful posters of the UKClimbing.com discussion forums for their invaluable feedback and advice, and also Evan and Natasha, for their support and patience.

References
1. Spread on the North Face of the Eiger uses information from *The White Spider*, by Heinrich Harrer.
2. Spread on Todd Skinner and The Nameless Tower uses information from Todd Skinner's website, *Beyond The Summit*:
http://www.beyondthesummit.com/exp_summ.html
3. Spread on Lynn Hill, Warren Harding and The Nose uses information from *Supertopo*, at supertopo.com
http://www.supertopo.com/

ISBN-13: 978 1 84898 139 3 pbk
This revised edition published in 2010 by *ticktock* Media Ltd

Printed in China
9 8 7 6 5 4 3 2 1

A CIP catalogue record for this book is available from the British Library.

Picture credits (t=top; b=bottom; c=centre; l=left; r=right; OFC=outside front cover):
4Corners images/SIME/Giovanni Simeone: 10/11t. Alamy/David Hosking: 9b. Aurora Images: 8 (Jose Azel), 33cl (Corey Rich). Josune Bereziartu: 14/15. Dave Bennet: 16/17t. Neil Bentley Collection: 37b. Boreal: 17cr. John Cleare: 4/5, 13t, 57b, 60t, 61t. Katherine Cooper: 2. Steve Crowe: 49cl. Cubby Images: 48, 49t. Chris Dainton: 52/53. Ged Desforges: 43t. Greg Epperson: 57t. The Fell and Rock Climbing Club: 12 inset. Graeme Gatherer: 19cl. Jack Geldard: 19b. Getty images: 18, 40/41t (Mike Powell), 47br (AFP), 51t (AFP). John Gill: 51b. Tim Glasby: 19t. Matt Hartgrove: 21t. Andrew Huddart: 43b. iStock: OFC, 1. Rob Lillywhite: 21cl. Josh Lowell: 44/45 (from the movie *King Lines*, www.bigUPproductions.com) 24/25 (from the movie *Dosage Vol IV*, www.bigUPproductions.com). Dave MacLeod: 46b. Chris McNamara: 56. Alex Messenger: 47bl. Bobby Model/M-11 Images: 55t. Gwen Moffat/S.R.G Bray: 13b. Frédéric Moix: 49cr. National Geographic: 6t (Getty Images), 54. Chris Noble: 50b. Peter O'Donovan: 38/39. Rich Potter: 17bl, 27bl. Galen Rowell/Corbis: 33t. Keith Sharples: 7c, 20, 23b, 32. Shutterstock: 3, 9t, 11bl, 19cr, 42, 46/47t, 58. Nick Smith: 22, 23t, 26, 27t, 28 all, 29 all, 30, 31t, 31b, 34, 35t, 36. Gordon Stainforth: 35b. Superstock/Age fotostock: 37t. Preston UtleyAP/PA Photos: 50t. Stewart Watson: 7t. Donald Willey: 12. Jörg Zeidelhack: 41t.

Every effort has been made to trace copyright holders, and we apologize in advance for any omissions.
We would be pleased to insert the appropriate acknowledgments in any subsequent edition of this publication.

CONTENTS

CHAPTER 1: BEGINNINGS

ROCK CLIMBING

British climber Joe Brown on Spider's Web, Gogarth North Stack, UK (1970).

OVERVIEW

Rock climbing is more than just a sport. It's about strength, balance and movement. It's also about learning how to use your body on the rock. Often, it's about keeping a cool head when you're afraid.

ROCK CLIMBING

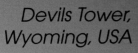

Devils Tower, Wyoming, USA

Sabine Bacher at the 2007 Climbing World Championship in Bulgaria.

Ben Moon climbs Big Bang, the Great Orme, UK

People climb all over the world. They climb everything – from small boulders to large mountain ranges.

Climbing is a dangerous sport.

If you want to learn to climb, check out your nearest climbing-wall gym. Instructors can teach you to climb as safely as possible.

Cave

A Dogon man climbs a cliff.

CLIMBING TO LIVE

Long ago, people climbed to survive. In a desert in Mali, Africa, caves can be seen on the face of a huge sandstone cliff. Thousands of years ago the Tellem people lived in these caves.

Today, the Dogon people live at the bottom of the cliffs. They climb the cliffs, searching the caves for forgotten Tellem treasures.

White House

The White House Ruins

The White House Ruins is an 800-year-old stone village in Arizona. The village was built high up on a canyon wall by the Anasazi people. They reached their homes by climbing or using ropes.

St Kilda

The St Kilda cliffs

People lived on the rocky islands of St Kilda, Scotland, until the 1930s.

The islanders ate seabirds. The seabirds lived on cliffs. The islanders had to climb the cliffs to catch the birds and gather their eggs.

THE FIRST MOUNTAINEERS

Powerful rulers sometimes ordered people to climb mountains. The rulers wanted to celebrate a victory or their gods. Sometimes they just wanted to show off.

Mont Aiguille is a gigantic rock in France. In the Middle Ages it seemed impossible to climb. It was known as 'Inaccessible Mountain'.

In 1492 the king of France commanded a soldier to climb the 'Inaccessible Mountain'.

The soldier, Antoine de Ville and his team used ladders and hooks to attempt the climb. It took several days, but they did it.

There are no easy ways to the top of Mont Aiguille, France.

In the 18th century people began to climb mountains for adventure.

Mont Blanc

In 1786 Italians Jacques Balmat and Michel Paccard reached the top of Mont Blanc. Mont Blanc is the highest mountain in Western Europe.

CLIMBING FOR FUN

In the 1880s Englishman Walter Haskett Smith started scrambling in the Lake District, UK. Scrambling is a mixture of climbing and walking.

Walter soon moved on to soloing rock climbs. Soloing means climbing on your own without ropes, ladders and spikes to protect you.

Napes Needle in the Lake District

Walter Haskett Smith made the first ascent of Napes Needle in 1886.

Joe Brown

The UK's Joe Brown was called the 'Human Fly' because he could cling onto very steep rock.

Joe Brown in the Wen Zawn area of Craig Gogarth, Anglesey, UK (1974)

Gwen Moffat climbing Superdirect, Wales, UK (1956)

Gwen Moffat

Gwen Moffat lived outdoors, sleeping under hedges.

Later Gwen hitch-hiked to the Alps and became the first British female mountaineering guide.

CHAPTER 2: BASICS

Spain's Josune Bereziartu is the world's top female sport climber. She climbed the ultra-hard Bain de Sang, Switzerland, in 2002.

STICKY RUBBER

Climbing boots are the most basic pieces of climbing gear. The boots are called 'stickies'.

The rubber they are made of moulds to the rock, helping the climber to grip.

Sole: Made of sticky rubber

Rubber strap: Helps shoe to keep its shape

There are different styles of boots for different sorts of climbing.

High-tech shoes squash the climber's toes. They are uncomfortable, so they are worn only during the actual climb.

Velcro straps: Quick to put on and take off

Loop: Helps the climber to pull on the boots

Ridged heel: For extra grip

Curved rand: Helps the climber to pull with their feet

Below is an all-round shoe. It is suitable for ordinary climbers.

A big wall shoe

An all-round climbing shoe is quite comfortable.

Big wall shoes are used for climbing mountain routes over several days. They are a cross between climbing boots and hiking boots.

CLOTHING

A climber's clothing should keep the climber warm and be worn in layers. Since climbing heats you up, layers can be removed to keep cool.

One of the world's top speed climbers, Indonesian Etti Hendrawati

Trousers

Climbing trousers should be flexible and give a clear view of your feet.

Duvet jacket

Climbers often get cold when they're at the bottom of the rock holding their partner's rope. A duvet jacket is full of goose feathers, so it is lightweight and warm.

Chalk

The bag a climber wears around their waist contains a type of chalk called magnesium carbonate. It helps climbers to grip by absorbing sweat from their hands.

Helmet

A helmet protects the climber's head in case they fall or are hit by rocks.

Pete Robbins
heel hooks on
Cromlech
Boulder, Wales, UK

CLIMBING MOVES

A heel hook gets one leg up high so that you can pull with your heel, like it's an extra hand. A heel hook helps to shift the weight from your arms to your leg when you're on steep ground.

This move is called an Egyptian.

Moving terms

- **Dyno:** Used when you can't reach the hold you want – so you jump to it.

- **Jamming:** Shoving a bit of your body in a crack so that it takes your weight with very little effort.

- **Smearing:** Moving up by placing the sole of the front of your foot flat against the rock.

A layback means the climber balances by pulling with his arms and pushing with his legs. It can be hard on your arms.

ROCK

A climber adjusts their style and technique to the sort of rock they are climbing.

Climbing on gritstone at Stanage Edge, Peak District, UK

Gritstone

Peak gritstone was formed from sand at the bottom of lakes and rivers around 300 million years ago.

Gritstone gives good grip for the climber's feet. It has round handholds, which climbers call slopers.

Limestone gives good handholds.

Limestone

Limestone is made from the bones and shells of tiny creatures that lived in the sea millions of years ago.

Tufa

Tufa is deposits of calcium carbonate. It can give big jugs.

Jugs are holds that come out from the rock. Jugs are easy to pull up on.

Jug

Climbing grades Climbing routes are graded by how hard they are to climb. The bigger the number, the harder the route.

CHAPTER 3: ROPED CLIMBING

American Lisa Rands was the first woman to climb E8-grade routes in the Peak District, UK. On these routes a fall could mean hitting the ground from over 15 metres.

CLIMBING PARTNERS

When climbers use ropes, they climb in pairs. The climber is tied to one end of the rope. The climber's partner is called the belayer.

The belayer holds the rope firmly all the time.

Belayer

The belayer is linked to the rope by a brake called a belay device.

This lets the belayer slide out rope as the climber goes higher.

The belayer stops the rope slipping if the climber falls off.

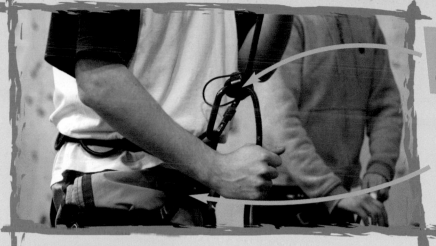

Belay device

Belay loop

Belay device

When the belayer holds the rope properly, the device creates a zigzag in the rope. The zigzag stops the rope slipping through it.

A climber wearing a harness.

Harness

A harness enables the climber and belayer to attach themselves to the rope. The waistband doubles back through the metal buckle.

Gear loops: Small plastic loops for hanging climbing gear when it isn't being used.

Leg loops: Strong bands that support the legs.

27

A climber places a wire in a crack.

TRAD GEAR

When climbing on natural rock, a climber uses gear to link their rope to the rock. Climbing this way is called trad climbing.

Cam

A cam is a mechanical device that is made smaller by pulling a lever. Then it is slotted into a crack. When the lever is released, the cam opens wider and wedges itself into the crack.

Wire

Wires are small wedges of lightweight metal, threaded onto strong wire. They slot into different-sized cracks.

Hex

A hex works like a wire, but it's bigger. It has six sides like a hexagon. It slots into bigger cracks.

Sling

Slings are straps of fabric tape formed into a loop. They are strong and secure.

Karabiner and quickdraw

A karabiner is an oval-shaped piece of metal with a hinged opening.

A quickdraw is two karabiners joined together. They link the gear to the rope.

TRAD ROUTE

When a climber gets ready to climb, they fasten their harness and attach their gear.

Then they tie the rope to their harness using special knots.

Leading

Once the belayer is ready, the leader begins to climb.

The belayer holds the rope that the leader attaches to the rock as they climb.

Placing gear

Climber with two pieces placed

The leader places gear and attaches the rope to it using a quickdraw. This means the belayer can stop them hitting the ground if they fall.

For the leader to be safe, they need to place gear well and often.

Second removing gear on the way up

Seconding

The leader fastens themselves to the rock at the top.

Their partner (second) stops belaying and ties onto the other end of the rope. Then it's the leader's turn to belay their partner.

*Steve McClure does
a bat hang in the
Yorkshire Dales, UK*

SPORT CLIMBING

**Not all routes have good places to put gear. Some
routes have bolts set permanently in the rock. A
climber carries quickdraws and clips them to the
bolts as they reach them. This is called sport climbing.**

ROCK CLIMBING

Warren Harding

Free climbing and aid climbing

Trad and sport climbing are types of free climbing.

In free climbing, a climber uses rope and gear to protect themselves in case they fall.

Beth Rodden climbing on a sport route

Trad climbing is when the rock face is left in its natural state and not bolted. This makes the route more dangerous.

A climber who is aid climbing puts metal objects into the rock and uses them for holds.

FALLING

When a climber falls, their life depends on their gear and their belayer.

A roped climber falls through the air

When a climber falls, the rope between them and the belayer suddenly pulls tight.

The bigger the fall, and the heavier the climber, the stronger the rope pulls.

Sometimes, gear has to be used to fasten the belayer to the ground.

Climbing rope is strong and stretchy.

Rope

Non-stretching, or static, rope cannot be used for climbing. Even a short fall on static rope can kill a climber.

A climber wearing a hemp waistband

Hemp

Before World War II, climbers used hemp rope. This was dangerous as hemp is not very strong and it is hard to undo when frozen.

MULTI-PITCH

If a rock is higher than the length of the rope, the climber must stop at a ledge. They then securely attach themselves to the ledge and belay the second climber up.

When routes don't have enough ledges, the lead climber attaches himself to the rock.

He hangs from the rock, whilst he belays the second climber up to join him. This is a hanging belay.

Each section of a route is called the pitch.

Sport

Multi-pitch routes are sometimes sport climbed, with bolts in place all the way up for protection.

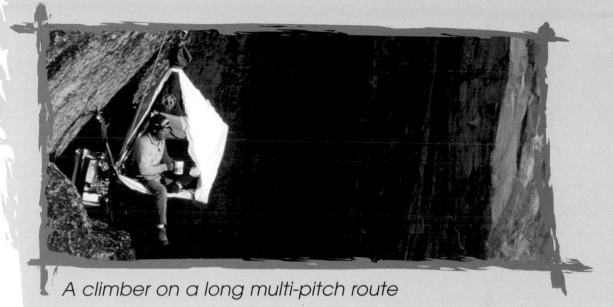

A climber on a long multi-pitch route

Portaledges

Some rock faces are too high to be climbed in one day. The climbers have to pull up bags containing food and fuel.

They sleep on artificial ledges called portaledges.

Portaledges must be secured to the rock so they don't fall down.

CHAPTER 4:

CLIMBING WITHOUT A ROPE

ROCK CLIMBING

Climber and mountaineer Andy Cave boulders in Wool Packs, Kinder Scout, UK.

The people at the bottom are ready to help protect the boulderer if they fall. This is called spotting.

BOULDERING

Climbing is not always about getting up high. Bouldering is unroped climbing on low rock. Bouldering routes are called problems.

Boulderers often use portable mats or pads to fall onto if they lose their grip.

Dai Koyamada on the Wheel of Life, Hollow Mountain Cave, Australia – one of the world's hardest bouldering problems

Dai Koyamada grew up in Japan. He made his own climbing wall inside his garage after seeing a photo of a climber.

These bouldering pads are folding mattresses made of special foam that is good at absorbing impacts.

Boulderers often like to climb in groups. They take it in turns to try challenging problems.

SOLOING

Soloing is climbing alone, usually without a rope. It is the riskiest form of climbing.

Risks of soloing

Even when a climber is on an easy route things can happen to make the climb more dangerous, such as:

- Slippery rock
- Loose handholds
- Rock falls

The south face of the Marmolada, the highest peak in the Dolomites

ROCK CLIMBING

The Fish

On 29 April 2007, Hansjörg Auer soloed a route known as The Fish, on the Marmolada in Italy. Hansjörg completed around 915 metres of extremely hard climbing in under three hours.

The Fish, Dolomites, Italy

A climber falls off a deep-water solo

Deep water

Deep-water soloing is soloing above water that is deep enough to break the climber's fall.

CHAPTER 5: ROCK STARS

American climber Chris Sharma was the first to climb a sport route with the high grade of 5.15a, in Realization, Ceuse, France.

ROCK CLIMBING

STRENGTH

Top climbers need to stay fit. They watch their diet and train their bodies to be as strong as possible.

The best climbers use climbing walls to keep fit.

Climbing walls hold competitions for climbers.

Climbers compete to see who can climb the hardest routes or problems. There are also speed-climbing competitions.

Dave MacLeod uses a finger board to improve his upper-body strength

The walls look like rock, or have holds that bolt-on.

Spain's Ramón Julián Puigblanque won the 2007 Rock Master competition in Lake Garda, Italy.

Ramón Julián Puigblanque

French climber Sandrine Levet winning the 2006 Rock Master competition

FIRST ASCENTS

The most famous climbers are those who climb the hardest routes.

*Scottish ciimber
Dave MacLeod
climbing on
Rhapsody, Scotland*

Dave MacLeod

In 2006, Dave MacLeod climbed the world's hardest trad route.

The route is Rhapsody, at Dumbarton Rock in Scotland.

British climber Dave Birkett made the hardest trad onsight climb in the world by climbing Fear of Failure in the Lake District, UK.

Onsight Climbing a route without practising on it beforehand or falling off.

TOP CLIMBERS

Most amazing young climber?

Bouldering is measured in V grades. The easiest boulder problem is V0. When she was only eight, American Cicada Jenerik climbed a V7.

Fastest climber?

Dan Osman was one of the fastest climbers ever. He soloed the 122-metre cliff, Bear's Reach in California, USA, in four minutes and 25 seconds. The average climber takes three hours on the route!

ROCK CLIMBING

Rising star

Born in 1990, Charlotte Durif was already the best female onsight sport climber by the time she was 15. She started climbing when she was nine.

Strongest climber?

American John Gill used gymnastics in rock climbing. He was the first person ever to pull himself up by just one finger.

CHAPTER 6:

LEGENDARY ROCK

ROCK CLIMBING

El Capitan, Yosemite
National Park, USA

THE TERRAIN

Rock routes often get as famous as the climbers who climb them.

The Nameless Tower

The Nameless Tower

The Nameless Tower is one of the Trango Group of rocks in Pakistan's Karakoram mountains.

The tower is almost 6,250 metres high. It rises a kilometre above the mountain ridge around it. It was first climbed in 1976.

Todd Skinner climbs the Nameless Tower

In 1995, American Todd Skinner gathered a team of expert climbers to free climb the east face of the Nameless Tower.

They planned to take two weeks to climb the upper wall. But difficult climbing and stormy weather meant they spent two months up there. Eventually they got to the top.

THE NOSE

El Capitan sits at the entrance to Yosemite Valley, USA. It rises 1,100 metres above the ground below.

In 1957, American Warren Harding decided to climb El Capitan. It took him and his companions 18 months to reach the top.

*El Capitan,
Yosemite, USA*

*A route to the
top, called
The Nose*

Lynn Hill

*Warren Harding reached
the top of The Nose in 1958*

During this time they climbed
up and down the rock face
over and over again. They
drilled bolts and attached
fixed ropes. These ropes were
left in place over the winter.

In 1993, Lynn Hill went
to El Capitan with
a dream. No one
had ever climbed
El Capitan free.

Lynn free climbed
The Nose in four
days! One year
later, Lynn free
climbed the
whole route in
less than a day.

THE OGRE

LEGENDARY ROCK

The North Face of the Eiger, or Ogre, in the Swiss Alps is one of the most famous climbs in Europe.

Toni Kurtz and three other men tried to climb the North Face in 1936.

*A railway line runs inside the Eiger; the tunnel has
a window looking out from inside the rock face*

At first all went well, but then the weather changed. The rock became covered with slippery ice. The other men were killed.

Rescuers tried to reach Toni through the train tunnel window. Toni's left arm was frozen solid by frostbite. He tried to reach his rescuers but died just before he got to them.

In 1938, four men, Anderl Heckmair, Heinrich Harrer Ludwig Vörg and Fritz Kasparek, reached the top of the North Face.

MILESTONES

1935 French boulderer Pierre Allain invents the first rubber-soled climbing shoes.

Pierre Allain

1945 Nylon rope replaces hemp rope, making falling off safer.

1958 Warren Harding aid climbs The Nose, El Capitan, Yosemite, USA.

1961 John Gill solos the Thimble, South Dakota, USA. It remains the world's hardest climb for over 15 years.

1970s Sport climbing is born in France.

1978 Ray Jardine invents Friends, the first cam.

1986 Johnny Dawes climbs Indian Face, Wales, UK – the first E9 trad route. It is so dangerous that it has been climbed only twice since.

1980s Crispin Waddy, Nick Buckley, Damian Cook and others invent and develop deep-water soloing on the coast of Dorset, England.

1991 Wolfgang Güllich climbs Action Directe, Frankenjura, Germany. It is still one of the world's hardest sport routes.

1993 Lynn Hill free climbs The Nose, regarded by most climbers as the greatest ascent of all time.

2000 Chris Sharma climbs Mandala, V12, in Bishop, California, USA – a steep boulder problem that had been considered a great project for many years.

2002 Josune Bereziartu climbs Bain de Sang, 9a, Switzerland – the hardest route yet climbed by a woman.

Wolfgang Güllich

Glossary

Aid climbing Using a rope and gear to pull yourself up the rock.

Ascent A climb to the top.

Belay device A rope brake used by a belayer to help them hold the climber if they fall.

Belayer The person holding the climber's rope.

Bolts Permanent protection fixed into the rock by drilling.

Boulderer A person who scales the lower section of rocks without a rope.

Bouldering Climbing fairly low down without a rope.

Cam A piece of equipment that is placed in cracks of the rock face. The climber attaches their rope to it during a climb.

Fixed ropes Ropes that are attached to the rock face and left in place to make retreat and later ascents easier.

Free climbing Climbing where a rope and gear are used only for protection in case the climber falls.

Gear The items a climber uses as they climb to help protect them in case they fall.

Gear placement Crack or place in the rock where protective gear may be slotted and to which the rope can be linked.

Leading
Climbing up the rock and clipping the rope to the protection in the rock as you go.

Pitch A section of a long climb.

Problem In bouldering, the route a climber takes in order to complete the climb.

Quickdraw Two metal ovals joined together by special super-strong fabric tape. They are used to link the rope to the bolt or gear in the rock.

Rand The rubber strip that runs around the bottom edge of a climbing shoe.

Route The way a climber goes as they climb up.

Seconding Following the leader up the rock face once they have reached the top, taking out any gear they placed as they led the route.

Sport climbing Climbing that uses bolts for protection.

Trad climbing Climbing where the rock face is left in its natural state and only temporary protection is placed.

Wire A chunk of metal gear that a trad climber places in a crack to help protect them if they fall.

Index